Copyright © 1971 by
Baker Book House Company

ISBN: 0-8010-5309-9

Library of Congress Card Catalog Number:
71-168382

First printing, July 1971
Second printing, December 1972
Third printing, October 1975
Fourth printing, November 1978

Printed in the United States of America

To those who seek exciting and enriching encounters with each other in their marriage relationships, we joyously dedicate this book. May God lead you to experience the greatest and most enjoyable fulfillment of life's powers, potentials and purposes.

Introduction

During the past nineteen years, God has given us the privilege of maturing together in Christian love and understanding. As our children have grown, we have come to realize that married couples can easily dwarf their spiritual lives if devotional experiences are kept at the children's level by mainly emphasizing family devotional periods. As maturing adults, we have needed much more than this. We have sought to grow by more intimate husband/wife devotional practices. We have chosen to study the Bible on an adult level, to agonize in prayer using adult terms, to spend time as an adult duet around the family organ, and we have found these things profitable.

But probably even more enriching than taking an adult approach to devotional experiences is following the his/hers approach. To enjoy a proper balance in the Christian home, both the male and the female perspectives must be expressed. This is true in relationship to Christian faith as well as what are often labeled as secular aspects of life. In relationship to our faith in Christ, we have endeavored to ask each other, "What does this particular Bible passage say to you?" or "How do you look at this situation?" The answers to such questions bring added depth to everyday husband/wife contacts.

Most devotional books have neuter flavor with a general appeal to either sex. Some, like *Devotionals for Modern Men* and *Dynamic Devotionals for Men,* two other Baker *Ultra* books that originated in our house, appeal to men who want their religion straight from the shoulder. Others are written exclusively for women.

In this book we take the his/hers approach. Subjects are placed in the his/hers sequence—first because we believe in the Biblical concept that the man is the head of the household—and secondly, to give continuity. In some instances, the female portion will contain the major thrust and should dominate the devotional experience. Each section is written to complement the other and should be read with this in mind. Each section should lead into the important "Let's Talk More" questions. We believe all devotional materials should have dynamic application to today's living.

The "Let's Talk More" sections challenge both partners to express additional ideas, to solve personal problems, and to enrich their marriage. We've discovered that talking together is the most helpful means for improving understanding. New dimensions in living appear when we have discussed specific questions. We're confident that you will also discover greater depths of Christian love through this process, especially if you make this a major aim.

We're excited about the idea of married couples sharing devotional ideas of an intimate nature and then discussing how they can improve their marriage by applying Christian principles to daily living. We only wish we could listen in as you use this book.

VILMA AND WILLIAM J. KRUTZA

Contents

I Am a Man/
I Am a Woman

When God created man,
He made him in God's likeness;
He created them male and female.

He blessed them
and called them human
at the time of their creation.

Genesis 5:1, 2 Berkeley

His

When God contemplated making the highest form of creation, He called him *Man*. After the account of creating minerals, vegetables, and animals, we read that God said, "Let Us make man in Our image, after Our likeness."

Man wasn't one among many creatures; he wasn't the highest accident of an unknown-what's-next evolutionary process. Man was God's noblest creature. It was as if God paused and proclaimed, "Let us make our most distinctive living creature—man!" Then God went about patterning man after His own personality. Now man possesses the image and likeness of God. It's great to be a man!

This has been dubbed "a man's world." Probably it's been that way since the Eden episode. The reasons are many, especially since the world of work requires the robust approach. Demands for success require bigness of heart, alertness of mind, dexterity of body. Meeting the challenges of today's demands requires the calculating abilities of a man. And an occasional flexing of muscles accomplishes a lot of heavy work that women could not perform.

Manliness also has its romantic aspects. God implanted female-drawing powers within males. One doesn't have to observe too many male/female situations to see this romantic power accomplishing its intended purposes. And most men retain their God-created sexual powers most of their lives. That's the way it ought to be.

But there are things that men won't and can't do. Likewise there are areas that are exclusively male territory. Happy is the man whose wife recognizes these in her husband and does everything within her womanly powers to promote the God-instituted male way of life.

10

Hers

From the scientific viewpoint, considering the intricacies of the female body, the divine act of bringing Eve into existence was a more delicate process than the creation of man. Notice that our text goes directly from "God created man" to "He created them male and female." There's no place for manly boasting about the man's designation. There was equality in creation.

Women certainly have to acknowledge that God's way of making Eve was a novel idea. Who but God would think of making woman somewhat like man by giving her a few of his parts. Woman is like man in many ways physically, emotionally, mentally and spiritually.

But women have some distinct characteristics. Baby production is a woman exclusive. From a small ovum fertilized by a man, a full-fledged person is developed—all within a woman's womb. Then there's female sensitivity that nurses child hurts and nourishes male pride.

Though many women work in the "man's world," there's still a place that can be called a "woman's world": home sweet home. God places the wife within the home to fulfill His purposes—in the kitchen, in the living room, in the family room, in the bedroom! She's in business—to keep husband and children happy. The mundane tasks of washing clothing, polishing furniture, bandaging skinned knees are performed in a spirit of love for her family.

Lest men think all romance begins and ends in the male column, a woman has powerful, God-created charms. Females don't have to do much to conquer the heart of a male. From this viewpoint, it's a woman's world. It's great to be a woman!

Only a few women want to take over mannish roles. Most women enjoy being feminine. And for the Christian woman there is a special joy in spending all of her time, abilities, energy, wisdom and creativity doing her own thing—being a pleasant, happy wife and mother.

11

Prayers

HIS

Lord, help me to maintain my manliness, both at home and in society. But in doing this, give me an understanding mind and a compassionate heart to discern how best to meet the needs of my wife. Help me to pattern my life after the Perfect Man, Jesus Christ. Amen.

HERS

Lord, help me to remember that I am a woman, that I have a continuous responsibility toward my husband to be a woman in every sense of the word. Grant that I shall be sensitive toward him. Grant me, too, contentment and joy as I perform the mundane tasks that can make ours a happier marriage. Amen.

LET'S TALK MORE

What can we do to improve our relationship so as to benefit each other during this week? In what ways can we better express our distinct roles and yet benefit each other?

Two Can Become One

Have you never read
that He Who made them
from the beginning made them male and female.
And said,
For this reason
a man shall leave his father and mother
and shall be united firmly
(joined inseparably)
to his wife,
and the two shall become one flesh?
So they are no longer two
but one flesh.
What therefore God has joined together,
let not man put asunder (separate).

Matthew 19:4-6 Amplified

His

Moving from the concept of the individuality of both male and female to "two can become one" requires more than a doctrinal statement. It requires both manly analysis and practical application. First must come a separation—"[he] shall leave his father and mother. . . ." It's interesting that this was not said to the woman. The untying of mother's apron strings seems to be more a man's problem than a woman's problem.

While God intends every man to be truly a man, and every woman to maintain her womanly role, yet there's a coming to-gether—a oneness, that can be realized.

Jesus said that the married man and woman are "united firmly (joined inseparably)." This inseparable union produces a oneness not known by unmarrieds. "They two shall become one flesh." This definitely has reference to the bodily and spiritual union of husband and wife in sexual intercourse. The height of that union is the oneness or orgasm—when husband and wife both experience the high ecstatic thrill of giving themselves to each other. To experience this profound thrill is the height of spiritual and physical pleasure between husband and wife. It involves intense physical, mental and emotional commitment.

God created the sexual act to be the most satisfying and intense physical intimacy and the most profound depth of mental and emotional oneness a married couple can experience. Jesus said that this was basic to marriage. And once that oneness is achieved, no man has the privilege or authority to break it. Since God created a man to so commit himself to his wife and a wife to so commit herself to her husband, Jesus proclaimed, "What therefore God has joined together, let no man put asunder."

This oneness of flesh is the most glorious way to express the individuality built by God into every man. The height of the sex act demands man's fullest concentration and creativity. Of course, it also takes loving cooperation from a wife.

14

Hers

This text is particularly applicable on the wedding day. Jesus said, "For this reason a man shall leave his father and mother and shall be united to his wife, and the two shall become one flesh."

To create an atmosphere—especially in the bedroom—where this two becoming one is a reality is a special challenge to a woman. It isn't simply a matter of being submissive, though that's involved. Submissiveness isn't synonymous with surrender. One can submit willingly; surrender usually implies that the victor has conquered the victim.

To participate in the body-thrilling sex act, a woman comes willingly and with the hope that she'll thoroughly satisfy her husband's need for total commitment of himself.

God has built a woman to also depend upon the sex act as a personal security. The satisfaction of her husband assures her of his commitment to her. The precious words, the gentle fondling, the ecstasy of orgasm all work together in telling her that her husband's love is genuine.

Beyond the recurring enjoyment of this act of oneness are the few special times when that oneness produces new life. There's an indescribable thrill when a woman can announce her pregnancy. She can joyfully proclaim that she is fulfilling God's command to multiply. The new life developed in her womb combines the physical, mental and spiritual characteristics of both herself and her husband. It's a oneness no man can put asunder. And what a thrill after the baby is born to hear others proclaim, "The baby looks exactly like you . . . him!"

Being joined inseparably to a husband is a wife's most satisfying experience.

Prayers

HIS

Thank You, Father, for the one who gladly took my name as her own. Give me the wisdom, the emotional aptitude, and the spiritual strength to deepen our oneness both in the sexual act and in all of our intimate relationships. Keep me from ever making these activities an end in themselves. Let them be a constant, consistent and enjoyable expression of our inseparableness. Amen.

HERS

O God, let the oneness that is expressed in our bedroom permeate the way we treat each other day by day. Help me to so express my emotions that my husband is drawn to me—for his benefit. Grant me the attitude of submission which turns all the hours we share together into hours of thrilling and satisfying activity. May I be constantly aware of my husband's sexual needs and make them a primary concern. Amen.

LET'S TALK MORE

What can each of us do to make the sexual act more of an expression of the oneness God seemed to have in mind for marriage partners?

What Is Love?

You who are husbands
must show love to your wives,
as Christ showed love to the Church
when he gave himself up on its behalf . . .
and that is how
a husband ought to love his wife,
as if she were his own body;
in loving his wife,
a man is but loving himself.

Ephesians 5:25, 28 Knox

His

Isn't it a backward approach to talk about oneness produced in the sex act and then to ask the question, What is love? Isn't the highly uncontrollable, happiness-impregnated, emotional sex act an act of love?

To find a definition of love satisfying to a man it might be well to consider what love *isn't* from the male viewpoint. A woman says, "I love that dress." That isn't love. She should have said, "I like." Love, being an emotion, relates to other emotional beings. A man *likes* a car, his house, a new necktie. Love involves persons.

We've all gone through the three meanings of love: *eros*—sexually stimulated love, infatuation; *phileo*—a companionship love; *agape*—a deep, unselfish interpersonal relationship. Agape expresses the type of love shown by God toward the world. Such love is other-centered. It is outgoing. It is concerned with the joy, contentment, happiness, well-being, and benefits of the person being loved.

Because of his fast-acting sexual response, man faces the great problem of determining what type of love he is expressing. Eros brings quick satisfaction. The companionship type, phileo, takes considerably more effort and is often not accompanied by eros. Agape often involves sacrifice—including the sacrifice of eros. Such love is the type a man will practice unconsciously. Whenever he becomes conscious of showing love, it usually gravitates into the other forms.

Eros and phileo are important for a well-balanced life. God made man that way. But possibly if more agape permeated the marriage relationship, the two others would receive better attention.

Hers

A woman often asks herself, even in the ecstatic experience of the sex act, What is love? Is this the highest form of love?

From an emotional point of view, especially when orgasm is reached, eros is the pinnacle. Who'd want more? But, in order to maintain this, one must go from one act to another. Of course, there's no complaint. God made woman to be unsatisfied without sex acts.

Another satisfaction accompanies the phileo love a wife can give to her husband. It's the kind she gives when he comes home discouraged. It's the kind that willingly listens to his complaints about lost sales, unreasonable employers, tangled traffic. It's the kind that offers an appropriate expression of comfort to fit each circumstance.

It's difficult to know when phileo lets off and agape begins. When does concern become so other-centered that it resembles the love of God?

One of the greatest joys a woman has is being able to detect when her husband needs a particular expression of love. Eros is needed at the appropriate time. Phileo should not be overlooked. Agape is an overall attitude—developed and fed by vital contact with Jesus Christ.

It's difficult to express love with no strings attached. Even to say "I love you" might imply "I want something" or "I did something of which you might not approve." Some females resort to such "love." It's neither eros, phileo or agape! Like men, women have to learn never to *use* love.

How womanly to employ all one's God-given emotions, physical and mental faculties, and will to express "I love you" to a husband. It's one of the great things God allows a woman to do!

Prayers

HIS

Lord, teach me the outgoing aspects of love, especially Your kind of love. Help me to recognize more situations in which I should express love—especially in situations which involve the one I prize most dearly. Amen.

HERS

In deed as well as in word, may my love be shown to You, to my husband, to my children, to others around me. Lead me to the realization that to love my husband is one of the most fulfilling acts I can perform. Amen.

LET'S TALK MORE

In what specific ways can we show more of the love of Christ toward each other? toward others in our community? Can we begin to do this consciously so we'll soon do it automatically?

Walking the Same Path

Do two
walk together
without being agreed?

Amos 3:3 Berkeley

Live in harmony with one another . . .
Don't become set
in your own opinions.
Don't pay back a bad turn
for a bad turn.

Romans 12:16, 17 Phillips

His

It doesn't take a mature married male long to discover that a woman doesn't think in male terms. A man values certain aspects of life; his wife values others. In fact, some masculine preferences are downright distasteful to a woman.

Take the man who loves auto mechanics while his wife is an immaculate housekeeper. She abhors the sight of greasy shirts, smudged sinks, blackened fingernails.

Should he give up his auto tinkering? Not necessarily. But he can practice the fine art of compromise. There's a good place to clean off dirty grease—at the basement sink.

Whether it's a job around the house or a philosophy of life, walking the same path is the only way to harmonized living. A husband's concern to bring about this harmony is essential. He'll have to say, "It's time we talk things over."

Talking over differences is one way to gain home harmony. It's no different from what happens at the office or in the factory. The employer talks things over with employees. Through this process jobs are designated, projects are completed, and people retain personal identity.

The New Testament portrays the church as an institution where people of varying opinions come together in a common fellowship. This can easily be adopted in a family setting. Paul didn't discount varying opinions, but he believed that harmonious living was possible in spite of them. Such living depends highly upon the Spirit's control of the individuals involved.

From the point of view of a man who constantly deals with varying opinions in his daily work, coping with such things at home ought to come easily. Unfortunately too many men become dogmatic, overbearing, and assume the role of the ruler of the roost. May God help such men to change.

Hers

Most married couples seem to forget the hand-holding sessions they had during courtship days. While casually walking down the street, if one tried to swing his hand forward while the other was taking a backward swing, disharmony occurred. And it was much easier to keep in step if there was harmonious arm-swinging.

Carrying this same attitude into all aspects of marriage makes for a tremendously enjoyable, challenging, and satisfying life. Agreeing to keep in step with each other, even while remembering there are distinct male and female shoes, makes for a happy and successful marriage.

Paul's words to the church are appropriate for the husband-wife combo. It's easy for a husband to become provoked when his wife doesn't "fall in line" to his pace or desires. Pouting comes quickly for a woman with sensitive feelings. And though being strongly opinionated is usually a male trait, females don't do too badly at it either. She can "pay back a bad turn for a bad turn," especially when she had all day to plan such subtle action. Just a little nastiness or a well-timed refusal to satisfy a husband's sexual desires—some crafty way to get back at her husband—while she smiles smugly to herself.

This harmony bit is a woman's task as well as a joint effort. No loving wife waits for a husband to compromise. She starts to walk his path and soon discovers it's an enjoyable one. Or she may discover a detour which they both will enjoy. Above all, walking the Jesus road makes both wife and husband happy. Agreeing and walking hand-in-hand with her husband is one of the biggest challenges a wife faces. For this, God led wife to husband and husband to wife. God still leads those who hold each other's hand tightly.

Prayers

HIS

All-knowing God, give me the insight to understand the intimate desires of my wife. Show me where we can dovetail our interests and walk closer together—more fully harmonizing our likenesses and our differences to fulfill better the purposes of our marriage. Amen.

HERS

Lord, help me to have a clearer vision of the path our marriage is taking. Give me the grace to go forward, to believe fully in my husband's choices, to be a helpmeet with ideas and attitudes as well as with work. May our marriage reflect the harmony developed by the Spirit of Christ. Amen.

LET'S TALK MORE

Name an area of life in which you as a couple have great harmony. What principles produce this harmony? Apply these principles to another specific area in which greater harmony is needed.

For Better or Worse

When others are happy,
be happy with them.
If they are sad,
share their sorrow.

Romans 12:15 TLB

His

It's not usually the nature of a man to express much joy or much sorrow. A man likes to laugh—but usually at what he calls the amusing things of life. Someone tells a joke and he responds with a hearty chuckle. An incongruity occurs in a situation involving either himself, a fellow worker, a friend, or a family member—he lights up with laughter.

But when it comes to expressing happiness, a man usually brings out his emotion-protection equipment. Why get all excited? Why become emotional? Why become frivolous? Something good or great has happened, acknowledge it and go back to normal living.

Show sorrow? Possibly. Shed tears? Never! That's just the way men are. Surely they feel sad in times of calamity. Surely sickness, accidents, death and disappointments bring sorrow to a man. But to express it—that's a sign of weakness. Why should a manly fellow cry? Of what benefit is a sad-faced fellow employee? Can a sorrow-filled father help his children overcome disappointments? Can such a husband bolster a sorrowing wife?

Most men have to admit they've developed a considerable amount of callousness. That's unfortunate. That isn't the attitude portrayed by the man's Man—Jesus Christ. He knew how to express happiness— He joined in celebrations with others. He also knew how to show sorrow—He viewed the inhabitants of the great city of Jerusalem as sheep without a shepherd, and wept.

It's true—the marriage situation is still the best place in which to express both of these emotions. Where else can one know so clearly the intimacy of another's feelings? Where else is such sharing needed more? "For better or worse" demands manly emotional responses.

Hers

How different women are than men. Emotions of joy bubble quickly; emotions of sorrow burst without reservations. Where you rarely have to tell a man to control his emotions, a woman needs reminders—especially if she's going to enjoy masculine approval. The average woman is constructed with her emotions close to the surface of her skin—easy to touch, easy to be touched off! Bring her into a joyous experience and she has the capacity to empathize with joy. Bring her into a situation of sorrow and she sincerely weeps.

Laughter is only one of a woman's happy expressions. She enjoys humor in the same way a man does. She's amused at incongruous situations. Home situations can easily turn into real life comedies, better even than those portrayed on TV. But happiness is more than chuckling and smiling. It's a feeling—an emotion. It produces an overall physical, psychological, and spiritual good feeling. It's spontaneous and deep within her personality.

Sorrowful situations produce similar reverse reactions: tears, emotional depression, possibly even physical pain, and spiritual and psychological anguish. It doesn't take much to make a woman cry. Tears often come without warning. Sobs may follow uncontrollably. Sympathy and empathy are close cousins. It's a woman's nature.

A wife can find no better person with which to fulfill Paul's command than with her husband. To be happy with him—sharing his laughter, joys and satisfactions. Then also when he is sad—to share his sorrow and disappointments. Ah, yes, God made women that way—to emotionally bubble and burst. Happy is the wife whose husband broadens his understanding of her meaningful emotional responses.

Prayers

HIS

God, penetrate my emotions until I spontaneously express both joy and sorrow. Make me less aware of reputation and more aware of the joy and sorrow of those around me. Help me to enter into both the better and the worse that comes into the life of my mate. Amen.

HERS

Thank You, Lord, for the womanly ability to freely express emotions. Help me never to use these expressions to attain selfish desires or unworthy aims, but to be always true to myself and to my husband. When happiness comes, may I share it; when sorrow comes, may I bear it—and thus show more of Your attitude. Amen.

LET'S TALK MORE

How can we further fulfill the sharing of the "for better or worse" aspects of our marriage vows during the coming weeks?

A Suitable Helper

The Lord God said:
It is not good
for the man to be alone;
I will make him a suitable helper,
completing him.

Genesis 2:18 Berkeley

His

Every man boasts about his choice of a wife—especially if he's pleased with the way she reacts to him. And every emotionally normal male seeks not only female companionship but also that one specific female whom he can call his own.

When God said that it wasn't good for a man to be alone, He knew what He was talking about. He created the male of the species with an incompleteness that could be completed only in the marriage relationship.

But Genesis tells us that God didn't simply make a sexmate. He didn't simply make one who'd enjoy the pleasures of the day or evening. She was made for a well-defined purpose—to be a "suitable helper."

Another translation says, "a helper fit for him." She was to fit into the life style of the man and to help him accomplish those purposes for which God designed Adam in the first place.

The account states that Adam named all of the creatures, but none could be found that was a suitable helper. All seemed to be motivated by instincts, not by intelligent, thought-out decisions. Thus God caused a deep special sleep to overcome Adam. Then God took one of Adam's ribs and formed the woman, whom He brought to Adam.

She was suitable because she possessed many of man's characteristics. She was suitable because she was especially made for him—mentally, emotionally, spiritually. She could join him in having dominion over the earth. There was no contrary purpose for the woman.

Man still draws "a suitable helper" to himself—to share his concerns, his tasks, his purposes—as God ordained. For this cause a man leaves father and mother and cleaves to a wife.

Hers

Every married woman deeply desires to fulfill her role as "a suitable helper." This designation has a physical meaning in and beyond the sex act. Proper and dynamic sex acts contribute to her husband's satisfaction. But she also uses all her physical and mental abilities and energies to make his home life comfortable and satisfying—she uses her housekeeping abilities, her culinary skills, her mental acuteness to keep herself and domain attractive to her husband. God made a woman this way and she's not really happy unless she fulfills that role. A suitable helper also helps her husband discover and develop his abilities to their full potential.

But there's also another point made in this verse. God made for Adam "a suitable helper, *completing him.*" Man is incomplete by himself. He's unable to function at 100 percent efficiency without a woman companion. That's the way God made man. A woman completes her husband in being a sex partner, in being a housekeeper, in being a mind expander, in being a ready sharer of joy and sorrow—being a complement to most of his life. Yes, any virile man is incomplete without a wife. Thus it's a healthy thing for a man to seek a wife.

When men evaluate each other, they usually utter the well accepted cliché, "Behind every successful man is a dynamic woman"— a suitable helper given by God to complete him. It's a joy for a wife to fulfill this God-ordained responsibility.

Prayers

HIS

Lord, I realize how incomplete I'd be without my wife's active participation in my life. Give me the spirit of appreciation that expresses itself not only in words, but in deeds. May she be happy that You brought her into my life as my suitable helper. Amen.

HERS

O Father, give me the humility to always accept my role as a helper to my husband. May I always be aware that this is Your intention for me. Keep me from intruding into those areas of his life that are peculiarly his—where I would be more of a hindrance than a help-meet. Give me joy and satisfaction as I fulfill the tasks of making him a complete person. Amen.

LET'S TALK MORE

In what ways can a wife be more of a helper to her husband in the home? in his business relationships? in community and church activities?

Love Your Wife / Love Yourself

Men ought to give their wives
the love they naturally have
for their own bodies.
The love a man gives to his wife
is the extending of his love for himself
to enfold her.
Nobody ever hates or neglects
his own body;
he feeds it and looks after it . . .
In practice
what I have said amounts to this:
let every one of you who is a husband
love his wife
as he loves himself,
and let the wife reverence her husband.

Ephesians 5:28, 29, 33 Phillips

His

For a man to say that he loves himself sounds conceited. It can also sound super-pious. It all depends on how he says it and how he acts after he has said it. Even the inflection of his voice may give away his inner attitudes. The only way to really understand the significance of Paul's statements about loving a wife as a man loves himself is to ask, "How does or how should a man love himself?"

True self-love isn't conceit. Conceit isn't love; it is haughtiness. A person "in love" with himself thinks too highly of himself. He thinks that he's better than others. That is conceit, not love. Self-love knows and accepts limitations of the personality. Weaknesses within are recognized, tolerated, and if possible, nurtured until strength appears. Sins are not excused, and although there is a recognition of the potentiality to continue sinning, there is also a desire to receive God's strength to resist evil.

Self-love maintains a healthy respect for the self. A man who loves himself knows his personal characteristics. He knows his abilities and attempts to improve them. He is also fully aware of his weaknesses and prayerfully struggles with them. He has assessed his moral fibre and desires to bring morality into his day-by-day life. He knows himself as a person—made in the image of God, a being far above animals.

Self-love attempts to reach out—to expand its influence. A man properly related to himself isn't selfish. He seeks the betterment of others. His talent and time aren't used only for self-gratification.

Translating self-love into wife-love—loving her like he loves himself: recognizing limitations without condemnation, recognizing strengths without jealousy, recognizing altruism without stinginess—all these show whether a fellow is truly the man God intended him to be.

Hers

A woman recognizes that her husband loves her like he loves himself when he gives unselfish devotion to her; when he's able to bypass her weaknesses; when he's able to bolster her strengths; when he's able to lead her into a fuller life.

Unfortunately not all women have husbands that love their wives as they love themselves. Some husbands compete against their wives. Others selfishly seek to get everything possible out of their wives. And then there are wives who reciprocate in a similar manner.

On the other hand, there's something extremely healthy and exciting about living in a situation where the husband has the proper attitude toward himself. It's a joy to be on the receiving end when a husband recognizes his weaknesses and takes a similar attitude toward those of his wife. Rather than condemning at every turn, he knows that in himself he also does wrong or insufficiently.

A man who has a healthy respect for his own body, mind and emotions will also have a respect for these in his wife. If he doesn't abuse his body, he won't abuse his wife's body or allow her to abuse herself. If he respects the powers of his own mind, he enjoys the productivity of his wife's mind and even challenges her to use it more. Knowing his own emotions, even though he might not allow them many outward manifestations, he understands his wife's emotional reactions—be they joyful, sorrowful, depressing, angry or. . . .

This is where eros and phileo part company. A husband who loves his wife as he loves himself isn't operating on the eros level. Here's where the impact of phileo—companionship love, understanding love, is felt the most. Here's where the "show me" love makes itself manifest in its most truthful forms—without being asked!

Prayers

HIS

I confess that much of my love of self has been pure selfishness. It has been nothing like the sacrificing, suffering, and serving love of Jesus Christ—the pattern for my self-love. Transform my attitude toward myself so I'll properly love my wife. Amen.

HERS

Too often I've looked for love in individual acts and misinterpreted the motivating forces of my husband's love, blaming what I thought were his self-interests rather than accepting his expressions on face value. Forgive me. Help me to create a climate in our home that will nourish his self-love. As he translates his attitudes toward himself over into attitudes toward me, give me the openness to accept these as true love. In the name of the loving Christ. Amen.

LET'S TALK MORE

In what ways can a husband's "self-love" be broadened and then manifested in practical ways in relation to his wife?

When Things Don't Go Your Way

Let there be no more resentment,
no more anger or temper,
no more violent self-assertiveness,
no more slander
and no more malicious remarks.
Be kind to one another;
be understanding.
Be as ready to forgive others
as God for Christ's sake has forgiven you.

Ephesians 4:31, 32 Phillips

His

All men have ideals—accomplishments they hope to attain in life. In their daily contacts these ideals are often frustrated. The actual rarely meets the ideal. So there's one last resort—set up ideals at home. Here the man, as head of the house, can work until his ideals are fulfilled. Here he can make demands that would not be acceptable in the outside world. The home—his private kingdom where he is king!

But even in the home ideals are rarely realized. Not because there's no desire for realization. Not because husband and wife can't agree. But simply because ideal-maker and ideal-fulfillers are human—100 percent so! Human frailities and mental limitations cause misunderstanding of goals and an inability to fulfill details to the nth degree.

From the human viewpoint, natural reactions could readily be: resent the fact that desires are unfulfilled, become angry with those with whom one lives, let tempers boil, assert yourself more demandingly and even violently, make malicious remarks to the one you love. Paul said that a man should do exactly the opposite of these. What he proposed doesn't come naturally!

To follow God's pattern when ideals are not attained or even trampled upon, to do as He has done thousands of times toward us—to forgive—isn't natural. How easy to react in hate-filled ways even to a wife whom a man loves. But Christ's way is: be kind, tenderhearted, understanding, forgiving. This requires a power beyond the man himself, the power of Christ invading the man's personality.

Then to begin over again, to set up new ideals, to trust Christ's power, to work with a mate, to forgive again, to patiently love and understand—that's what makes Christian marriage so much different!

Hers

Resentments can quickly build up in the mind of a wife. She sees the attention her husband gives to women in his business contacts and compares this to the nonchalant way he treats her. She notices the careful ways he performs his salary-collecting tasks and how sloppily he does work around the house. She spends several hours preparing a special food treat and he barely says thanks.

Since a woman's emotions seem near the surface, these emotions are quickly hurt. Anger can readily develop. Why doesn't he pay more attention to her? Why can't he do his fair share of the work around the house? Why isn't he more appreciative?

From a woman's viewpoint, resentments, anger, and self-assertiveness just to get a proper amount of a husband's attention—aren't these justified?

But to be kind to a husband—that's a wife's joy. To understand that he has many problems on his mind, to understand that he treats other women on a business basis and reserves his love for his wife—that's a wife's prerogative. To accept the fact that he is going to be unexpressive at times, even when the food is scrumptious—all these require grace bestowed by God.

To be kind to a weary husband. To be understanding to a perplexed husband. To be forgiving to a husband who portrays the natural man's characteristics that Paul refers to in this verse. A Christian wife must do all these—because she has been forgiven by God. Forgiving her husband is one of the most healthy psychological and spiritual exercises a wife can perform. And isn't it marvelous to pattern one's attitude toward a mate on the basis of what God has done through Jesus Christ—forgiven us!

Prayers

HIS

The world is too filled with resentments, angry men, and violent demonstrations for me to join them. Lord, forgive me when these things crop up in my personality. May I display kindness, love and understanding in my home so as to make it a place where my wife, children and friends find their greatest enjoyment and fulfillment. In the name of the One who knew life's greatest abuses, even Jesus. Amen.

HERS

Realizing that my husband's working ideals are often frustrated, give me the inner power to fulfill those ideals we have prayerfully established at home. Help me to have the mind of Christ in analyzing the activities and attitudes of my husband. May I make our home a place where kindness, understanding, and charity are permanent residents. Amen.

LET'S TALK MORE

What specific areas in our lives still need to be brought under the categories of kindness, understanding and forgiveness? How can we accomplish these this week?

Flunking the Love Test

Love is so patient
and so kind;
Love never boils with jealousy;
It never boasts,
is never puffed with pride;
It does not act with rudeness,
or insist upon its rights;
It never gets provoked;
it never harbors evil thoughts;
Is never glad when wrong is done,
But always glad when truth prevails;
It bears up under anything,
it exercises faith in everything.
It keeps up hope in everything.
It gives us power to endure in everything.

I Corinthians 13:4-8 Williams

His

Ask any man, "Do you love your wife?" and he'll answer affirmatively. He might even challenge the questioner, "Why ask? Can't you *see* that I love my wife?"

The criteria that society has established as a test for husband-for-wife love includes providing adequate financial means to maintain a comfortable home, sufficient groceries and clothing, and security in the future by means of a retirement program and insurance; fidelity—loyalty to wife and children, no two-timing when away at conventions or at the office; taking part in reasonable amounts of entertainment and family togetherness; being reasonably compatible in everyday relationships, being neighborly and a good host.

Any man worth his salt meets these requirements. Such a man would be rated "good" or "excellent" in the husband column. Probably most men would say either that they pass the test or are attempting to better themselves in the ratings.

But when a man compares his relationship with his wife with Paul's scoring sheet, Wow! The score usually plummets. If he answers every question honestly, he's almost afraid to look at the grade on the test sheet.

Why is it that we so readily pass the test of what men think love means, but have so much difficulty with God's test? Because it's difficult to be patient, kind, never jealous, never boastful, humble, tender, etc., with a wife. Yes, it's difficult to develop those characteristics in the home—especially if a man hasn't practiced them often. But being related to God through Christ ought to implant more of the true characteristics of love. There's hope then. A man can ask the Lord, and his wife, to help him become the loving person he ought to be. Almost immediately he'll get a passing grade on the love test!

Hers

According to what Paul writes in this text, love seems to center in the will of the person. And women have the tendency to express love more by emotions than by deliberate willful acts. That's the nature of women. Of course, one shouldn't divorce emotions from love. Who'd want to?

Women, likewise, have set up certain societal standards by which they tell the world of a wife's love for her mate: feeding him tasty meals; keeping him well clothed; being an enjoyable sex partner; fidelity; sharing his tensions and enjoyments; instilling in his offspring respect and love for him; not a gadabout or a flirt.

Somehow society has also related the love chapter a little more to women than to men. Women are expected to have some of the characteristics mentioned by Paul as signs of maturity and motherhood. A woman is expected to love husband and children—or at least the children.

How well does the average woman do on the love test? Patience, kindness, not glad when wrong is done—all these virtues are easier to display as a mother than as a wife. Some women feel that when children are involved she has to express some of these characteristics, otherwise neighbors and friends will think she is an inadequate mother. But displaying such virtues in her relations with her husband doesn't seem so important to her. Of such a wife you might hear a man say, "I'm glad *I* don't live with her!"

Taking each point of the love test and making it a test for marital happiness is something each husband/wife team needs to do. The results will be unbelievable. And a woman's inner being responds with an ever expanding love and personality development when these characteristics become evident. Probably a man would respond likewise. Ought not all of us give it a giant-sized try?

Prayers

HIS

Loving God, who loved me while I was yet a sinner and even while I continue in sin, forgive my unloving ways. Implant Your Spirit deeper within my personality so I'll love more openly and more honestly — even as You love. Amen.

HERS

Help me, God of love, to see that love has ever expanding facets that can be employed in my home relationships. Give me the spirit of excited expectancy to see how my husband will respond to some deeper characteristics of love. In the name of the totally loving Christ. Amen.

LET'S TALK MORE

How can we more specifically show our love for each other without necessarily stating that we are doing so?

The Third Partner in Marriage

What God then has joined,
man must not separate.

Matthew 19:6 Berkeley

For where two or three
have gathered in My name,
I am there
with them.

Matthew 18:20 Berkeley

His

We know that no Christian marriage is complete unless it is a triangle—with a husband and wife at the two equal lower points at the base and with God at the pinnacle. We believe firmly that it is God who joins Christians together in marriage. God blesses the Christian marriage and home. Yet, after months or even years of marriage, having God as the third partner often seems undefinable.

How to take God into account in every situation is not only challenging but also sometimes confusing. How does He fit into the nitty-gritty of life? What place should He have when the man is considered head of the household? Should a man first discuss problems and plans with God and then turn to his wife? Or should they discuss such things on the human level before seeking divine assistance? Or should they develop some type of mystical relationship where it is a threesome? Would that threesome be man/wife/God, God/man/wife or man/God/wife?

Matthew's verse about gathering together in Christ's name relates mostly to a church group made up of unrelated people. But it could be related to the marriage situation. A married couple fulfills the "two gathered" criterion. And surely some of the most intimate spiritual experiences are developed and shared in the bonds of marriage by husband and wife.

When a Christian couple comes together in Christ's name, He's there. The triangle is complete. Probably the best way to discuss problems then is as a threesome, surely recognizing the contributions of each other on the human level, but immediately asking the Lord, "What do You say?"

Of course, being head of the house, it's a man's responsibility to instigate the action and keep the conversation going.

Hers

Even before she took the wedding vows, the Christian woman realized that God intended that marriage be permanent. Bound together by God, come what may, she plans her future accordingly. But as she plans she finds it is so easy to ask God about what's right after either making up her own mind or discussing subjects with her husband. And that's poor planning.

A look into the New Testament gospels soon convinces any person that God is concerned about common situations of life. Jesus constantly mixed everyday affairs into His teaching. He touched people who were sick, He attended family feasts and funerals, He talked to fishermen or tax collectors. Yes, He was interested in the nitty-gritty.

It might be more natural for a woman to consult God for help than it is for a man to do so. Men are notoriously self-sufficient. Women, being dependent upon men, also show a greater dependence upon God. Looking up to Him can be as natural as looking straight forward to a husband.

How wonderful to experience the mind of Christ by committing a situation to His understanding and care. His Word provides principles to follow and examples of others who have found divinely-prompted answers. And a woman enjoys the security of having answers.

Sharing these experiences with a believing husband deepens a wife's belief in God. So the triangle, in which God is always recognized as supreme, but in which husband and wife talk things through and pray about them, makes marriage stronger and complete. How good for a wife to ask, during conversation with her husband, "What does God say about this?"

Prayers

HIS

Lord, since I see only one partner in our marriage, I sometimes forget that You are around. Alert me to the great importance of maintaining an open line of communication with Yourself. I pray this especially for the benefit of the one You graciously brought into my life and whom I enjoy as a life partner. In the name of the communicating Christ. Amen.

HERS

Lord, it's often easier to run to You with my problems than to share them with my husband because it's easier to admit to You that I need help than it is to him—and because I trust Your answers more than I trust his. Give me the courage to share my problems with him so I can then more intelligently share them with You. May we find greater satisfaction in adopting Your solutions to our problems and Your principles to our plans. Amen.

LET'S TALK MORE

Do any areas of life exist in which we have left God out of the planning? Why? What can we do to change this approach and sense His purpose for us in all aspects of living?

Accomplishing Common Goals

Again I tell you,
if two of you on earth agree
(harmonize together, together make a symphony)
about—anything and everything—
whatever they shall ask,
it will come to pass
and be done for them
by My Father in heaven.

Matthew 19:19 Amplified

His

Goal setting is an integral part of any industrial society. Goals are set regardless of what form of government exists in an industrialized country. Advancement over last year's accomplishments is planned. So we are made aware of goal setting because it is a part of our national stance in the world. National goals soon filter down to local levels. Manufacturing firms fit into the scheme. And each employee of these manufacturers is challenged to set certain goals, and then is expected to accomplish them.

Personal goal setting has also been woven into other aspects of society. Be a better person. Develop greater skills. Acquire more leisure time. Develop greater financial security. Enjoy more entertainments. Materially, goals become important to the person—purchase a new automobile, a larger house, more up-to-date furniture, work-saving appliances, better clothing. . . .

To bring goal setting techniques into a marriage doesn't call for any revolutionary thinking. Nor does it in any way negate the man's responsibility to God or to his wife. In fact, God seems to bless families that have defined goals.

Looking at life from the male point of view might cause some conflict in goal setting in marriage unless there is compromise. Conflicts can be tempered considerably if more of the goals are of a spiritual and psychological nature than material nature—although there needs to be harmony on this important matter, too. Life can't be lived without material things, but they must not dominate.

Spiritual goals can't be defined as readily, but they must be developed. And it's a man's task, as head of the house, to begin the development of such goals. He has the responsibility to lead his wife and children into greater Christlikeness. Let's begin today.

Hers

Let's begin at the point Matthew stated: let's harmonize. Making a symphony requires that both partners play their proper notes—different, but harmonious. Perhaps there is more disharmony and discord at the marriage level, even in Christian homes, than at any other level in society. That may be one reason why James talked about wars and fightings among the believers!

Why is it that in business people seem to be able to define goals, but in marriage so few are spelled out? Why is it that with outsiders we accept specified goals and even the means of accomplishing them, but at home we live with little purpose in mind? Why do so many Christian couples have no goals, do not symphonize together and thus do not enjoy the fulfillment of shared ideals and ideas?

Perhaps this is an aspect of married life where the wife can in a special way be a help-mate for her husband. Because she is so involved with the family unit, she may be able to see needs not so obvious to her husband. She may be able to suggest goals and often is the one who must implement them.

For many, the last phrase of this verse doesn't seem very real: "It will come to pass and be done for them by My Father in heaven." This is where the Third Partner of the marriage comes in. What a dynamic! God accomplishing what we plan—it sounds unbelievable!

Let's not get bogged down with too many goals. That would be unrealistic. Choose about five long-range goals—things that a couple could accomplish within five years. Have about five medium-range goals—to be accomplished in six to twelve months. Several shorter-range goals should be set for near immediate fulfillment.

To accomplish goals takes more than planning. It takes cooperation. It takes the masculine qualities of leadership and discipline. Add the feminine qualities of imagination and perseverance plus the blessing of God and success is assured.

Prayers

HIS

Divine Planner, inspire me to see the worthwhileness of having specific goals. Give me the wisdom to plan such goals with my wife. Then give me the energy and discipline to accomplish them, relying on Your power. I pray this for Your glory and for our enjoyment and benefit. Amen.

HERS

Lord, I need more of the ability to accept goals and then to work creatively and with perseverance toward accomplishing them. Give me the inner spirit that drives me to accomplish the goals we have prayerfully established. In the name of the One who accomplished the greatest known goal—providing salvation for sinners. Amen.

LET'S TALK MORE

What specific goals do we have in life? What goals do we have for this year? List these in two columns. What new goals should we set? List these and also list suggested ways to accomplish them.

Continuous Forgiveness

Then Peter came to him and asked,
Lord, how often
must I see my brother do me wrong,
and still forgive him;
as much as seven times?
Jesus said to him,
I tell thee to forgive,
not seven wrongs,
but seventy times seven.

Matthew 18:21 Knox

Accept life,
and be most patient and tolerant
with one another,
always ready to forgive
if you have a difference with anyone.
Forgive as freely
as Christ has forgiven you.
And, above everything else,
be truly loving.
for love is the golden chain of all the virtues.

Colossians 3:13, 14 Phillips

His

When living or working with one person over a period of time, especially if one is married to that person for several years, it's not difficult to discover that person's faults. Often a wife's faults clash with a husband's strengths—then arguments can crop up.

"Forgive me," she cried after she scorched his best shirt. "Forgive me," she cried after she burned the roast on the evening important business guests were to arrive for dinner. "Forgive me," she cried after she dented the new car's front fender only eleven days after he proudly drove it home from the automobile dealer's showroom. "Forgive me," she cried when she emerged as beautiful as ever, but late, from her dressing room to attend the company's formal banquet.

What else could he say to her but, "Yes, Honey, I forgive you." But in his mind another thought kept repeating itself—a sentence he almost blurted out, "But don't do it again!"

Surely there's no wrong in hoping for the day when a marriage partner will do things in such a manner as to get constant approval rather than needing continual forgiveness. But most likely that time will never come—for either the wife or the husband. Both are all too human.

How many times must a man forgive his wife? Why ask? Jesus really meant that a person ought always to be forgiving. And for a man to do this sincerely requires not only tender loving care, but also a great deal of honesty. When a man says "I forgive" it has to go deeper than words. Only God can give him the patience, tolerance and true love that couples a forgetfulness of mind with forgiving words. Surely the pattern is an exalted one—forgive as freely as Christ has forgiven you. Most men have a long way to go—but striving to attain this goal surely would improve marriage relationships.

Hers

It isn't so difficult for a wife to forgive her husband if the offenses are varied and don't involve moral issues. But when a husband continually repeats a wrong, then a wife is tempted to ask, "How many times must I forgive him?"

Of course, the words of Christ are plain. Forgive an unnumbered number of times. That's pretty close to what Paul said when he told the Colossians to "forgive as freely as Christ has forgiven you."

Forgiveness, to be complete, requires a high degree of forgetfulness. Possibly one can never erase a thought from her mind, but forgetfulness in the practical sense means never to bring up a matter in an accusing way again. That's difficult. It's very tempting to bring up past offenses at a time when you are reviewing new ones. Words often slip. Accusations become heated. Support from the past seems to be one of the best ways to dramatize a fault in the present.

Isn't this one reason a husband and wife have to maintain spontaneous and honest communications? They have to trust each other. Then when wrongs are performed, either consciously or unconsciously, the offending partner can ask for forgiveness and the offended one can freely give it. There's joy in forgiving one another—because there's joy in experiencing a mended relationship. Besides, this is Christ's pattern for loving living. One can't go wrong in following His advice!

Prayers

HIS

Thank You for the forgiveness expressed through Your cross. Make me aware of how I offend others—especially my wife. Give me the humility to say "Forgive me," and the power not to offend. May love make me more genuine in my forgiveness of others. Grant me, too, the ability to forget a forgiven offense. In the name of the One who cried, "Father, forgive them for they know not what they do." Amen.

HERS

Make me aware of how I offend others . . . especially my husband. Lead me to forget the times I have forgiven my husband for wrongs committed. May I always be ready to forgive regardless of the offense. In freely forgiving and forgetting, may I show the depth of the love of Christ. Amen.

LET'S TALK MORE

For what do you really not want to forgive me? Why? How can we incorporate more forgetfulness into our forgiveness?

Sexmates

How beautiful are your feet in sandals,
O maiden of queenly form!
Your rounded thighs are a jeweled chain . . .
your navel is a rounded bowl
in which mingled wine is never lacking . . .
Your breasts are as two fawns,
the twins of a gazelle. . . .
How beautiful you are, my love,
how lovely in that which delights! . . .
Your breasts shall be as clusters of vines,
the fragrance of your breath as of apples.
The roof of your mouth is like red wine
flowing down for my beloved with smoothness . . .
I belong to my beloved,
and his desire is for me.

Song of Solomon 7:1-3, 8-10 Berkeley

His

It appears that God took the human sex act for granted right from the beginning.

Most likely this was based upon the fact that most living things openly engaged in sexual activities—and in the Garden things weren't any different for Adam and Eve. They did what came naturally, as naturally as for flowers, insects, beasts. And as far as we can surmise, they probably enjoyed every moment of it. God intended it that way!

The Bible does not give specific instructions about participation in sexual intercourse. But the negatives—the prohibitions—lead one to conclude that the sex act has been important to all civilizations. All the laws governing sex were made to protect the husband/wife relationship from perversion, the strongest of these negatives being written into the Ten Commandments: Thou shalt not commit adultery.

Since God has made us sexually potent, then it seems logical to conclude that sex relations ought to be high on the list of husband/wife activities. Partners ought to devote considerable creative energy in preparing for satisfying, entertaining sex acts. Each should understand the makeup of his mate's body and emotions and seek each other's highest satisfaction. Each should understand the intricacies that go into enjoyable coitus. Together they should seek mutually exciting and satisfying intercourse.

And though such relationships are kept guarded as secrets of their marriage, together a couple can formulate their own reactions to each other much as Solomon did in his Song. That's one reason God made sex important from the beginning.

Hers

Can a husband ever understand fully the importance of the sex act in the life of his wife? Though he usually makes the first advances, still sexual intercourse remains life's greatest physical and emotional enjoyment for her as well. The communication upon the bed brings a wife into a wonderful, unique, quite unexplainable, yet enjoyable, relationship with her husband.

As Solomon portrays the delights a man has in the intimate sex relationship, so can a woman ditto his phrases. She wants to be as sexually attractive as possible—to fulfill that wonderful role of being a sexmate. She does everything possible to entice her husband into an intimate encounter.

The gentle caressing and intimate fondling, these give her a sense of her husband's love. She appreciates being handled considerately. She reciprocates her husband's emotional responses. She wants to satisfy his sexual thirsts. A Christian woman recognizes that God constructed her body so it would be attractive to her husband.

There aren't any specific Scriptural instructions on how to act in the master bedroom, but Christian attitudes ought to be exercised also—more correctly, "particularly"—in the intimacies of marriage. Nowhere can a woman give herself in more complete abandon than to her husband in this most intimate act. And it is upon the marriage bed that husband and wife often reveal their innermost attitudes—and stand to be hurt the most deeply. It's no wonder, then, that God condemns so severely the defilement of the marriage relationship. Being a pure sexmate is a valuable Christian endeavor. To accomplish this a wife devotes much thought and continual submission to her loving husband. And she seeks to develop those attitudes which most fully express the intimate love that God incorporated in the physical and emotional makeup of the woman in the Garden.

Prayers

HIS

Lord, help me to understand the sexual makeup of my wife and to do everything within my God-created powers to satisfy her desires. Lead us to greater enjoyment of our sexual acts. In the name of Him who purposely created us male and female. Amen.

HERS

Dear God, let me fulfill more of what the man of wisdom said about my body's importance in the sexual experience. May we so enjoy each other's bodies that our oneness takes on its highest ecstatic forms. Amen.

LET'S TALK MORE

Are each of us fully satisfied sexually? How can we improve this aspect of our marriage? In what ways does our Christian faith influence our sexual acts?

Sacrificing Personal Rights

The husband should give his wife
what is due to her as his wife,
and the wife should be
as fair to her husband.
The wife has no longer
full rights over her own person,
but shares them with her husband.
In the same way
the husband shares
his personal rights with his wife.

I Corinthians 7:3, 4 Phillips

His

Paul says that "the husband should give his wife what is due to her as his wife." This can be quite a large order. Who is to determine what is due to a wife? Should the wife or the husband decide upon the listing? If a husband decides, will the list be comprehensive? If the wife decides, will the list be too demanding?

If we go at it from either of these points of view, we'll never make an adequate list. Thus Paul sets forth the tempering criteria concerning personal rights of wife and husband. He places them on an equal footing. What a husband owes to his wife is gauged by the sharing of personal rights. This involves what most men do not appreciate—compromise. It involves yielding to the preferences of a wife. It involves doing for a wife what a man would like his wife to do for him. Paul says that a man should pay particular attention to his wife's needs and desires and place these above his personal needs and desires. This is the route of love.

The apostle Paul had an uncanny way of stressing Christian principles for marriage partners. He must have clearly understood the attitudes of Jesus Christ who advocated the "two-mile hike" approach to living. He didn't take the cultural approach that downgraded women. Rather, Paul based the marriage relationship upon mutual respect and love.

Above all else, love is due to a wife. And this must be deliberately expressed—even above personal rights. As important as personal rights are in American society, others' (in this case, a wife's) rights come first. Thus the good of his wife becomes a man's highest home goal. And in meeting this goal he thoroughly satisfies himself. That's the way God ordained that it would work out.

Hers

One of the greatest faults of the women's liberation movement is its utter disregard for Biblical principles. A woman does not enjoy the privilege of dominating a husband. As Paul clearly states here, "The wife has no longer full rights over her own person, but shares them with her husband." This does not mean that she becomes a plaything or a household slave. In giving up her rights over her own person, she does not become less than a person. On the contrary, she shows the maturity of her womanhood.

The key here is not "unwilling surrender," but "loving submission." There's abundant freedom in voluntary submission. A woman in love knows the values of submission. She also knows how to share. A wife who loves her husband shares the intimacies of her person with him.

"In the same way the husband shares his personal rights with his wife." Such marriage is not only a legal, but a love, relationship. A woman is never complete until she shares the most intimate aspects of her personality with a loving husband.

We have a tendency to hold back because we somehow fear, often wrongly so, that we'll be dominated. This is especially a female fear. Because history is so full of examples of women being assigned to roles less than human, women quickly fear a return to such a situation if the male doesn't make the proper approach.

But Paul didn't place this reservation in this text. He was speaking to Christians. So as Christians, a husband and wife need to share fully what they'd otherwise keep for themselves. Getting into the innermost part of a husband's life is a joy reserved for a loving wife. And surely the converse is true.

Prayers

HIS

Lord, You never seemed concerned about Your personal rights. Help me not to be so concerned about mine, especially in my home where I know that to share and to sacrifice my personal interests is for the good of my marriage partner and our marriage. May my wife's personal good be one of the strongest desires of my life. In the name of the love-sharing Christ. Amen.

HERS

Help me, O Lord, to have the security that trusts my husband not to take advantage of my submission to him. As I share my rights and innermost thoughts with him, may I become a constant source of encouragement, education and vitality in his life. Amen.

LET'S TALK MORE

What hinders us from sharing more of our personal rights with each other? How can these hindrances be removed?

Enjoying Your Partner

Enjoy life
with the wife you love
all the days of the passing life
which He grants you under the sun.

Ecclesiastes 9:9 Berkeley

Derive delight
from the wife of your youth . . .
be always infatuated with her love.

Proverbs 5:18, 19 Berkeley

His

There's a tremendous amount of drudgery in life. Ask the average man if he is enjoying his job. He'll answer, "Are you kidding?" Take a good look at the average housewife. Judging from outward appearances, she's not enjoying, she's "enduring"—and not too successfully at that! Very few people seem to be able to smile about the majority of things they do. The normal pattern seems to be more an "endure life" style than an "enjoy life" manner. So why should marriage be any different? Yet the writer of Ecclesiastes and the wise composer of Proverbs come along with the idea that a man ought to enjoy life with his wife. The Ecclesiastes' writer said this is possible "all the days of the passing life which He grants you under the sun." The writer of Proverbs might be referring to more youthful days. And in many cases it appears that enjoying a mate somehow terminates with the falling out of or the graying of hair.

Maybe it's a man's fault. Quite often he limits enjoyment of a wife to indulging in her good food, watching television with her, or the sex act in the bedroom. But there's much more to enjoying a mate: the mental stimulation, the emotional satisfaction, the challenging of the will brought forth by intimate and intelligent communication; the sharing of an understanding of God's Word and will; the investigation of new potentials of life. Ah, life with a wife can be extremely enjoyable—even to being "always infatuated with her love." So, if a male mate is to enjoy his female mate (or vice versa) all the days of his life, he'd better begin it today. Otherwise he'll have to "derive delight from the wife of his old age." And that isn't quite what God intended. Besides, by that time he won't know how!

Hers

We live in an era when enjoyment seems to center in things rather than in people—especially the people with whom we should have our most intimate fellowship. We enjoy air-conditioned automobiles, convenience-packed homes, cooked-by-others meals. We listen to high quality stereophonic music, watch color-perfected television. And though we nominally participate in most of these activities with those we love, the emphasis is more on the thing than upon the person with whom we are enjoying the thing.

Most of us really don't know how to enjoy each other. We even have a tendency to use each other as things. Or, when the opportunity arises for stimulating activity, we don't know what to suggest. We still think of things. So these verses challenge us (and you can readily substitute "husband" for "wife" in both cases) to a different type of enjoyment—an enjoyment of the personhood of a mate.

To enjoy a mate as a person requires an interchange of ideas, be they lofty, intellectual thoughts or emotion tingling suggestions. Such ideas can come in "think" sessions or in quiet, relaxing "hold-your-hand" hours. And some of the most intimate communications can be related through the sensitivity method—a simple touch or a kiss.

Unless mates plan to have specific enjoy-each-other sessions, they probably won't. There's too much routine, too much drudgery to occupy the time.

God made a husband and a wife to enjoy each other. Happy is the man and the woman who take advantage of this God-originated arrangement.

Prayers

HIS

Lord, You promised abundant life to Your followers. Mine is so often lived in a near-famine state even in relationship to my mate. Lead us into fuller enjoyment of Yourself, of our partnership, and of the world around us. Amen.

HERS

Guide me, Lord, into a life that finds its enjoyments in communication with Yourself, my husband, and others. May my mind center in persons more than in possessions. I too seek the abundant, enjoyable life You talked about. In the name of the life-providing Christ. Amen.

LET'S TALK MORE

In what ways can we enjoy each other more? What hinders that enjoyment? How can we rectify the situation?

Taking a Two-Mile Hike

You have heard that it was said,
An eye for an eye
and a tooth for a tooth.
But I tell you
that you should not offer resistance
to injury;
If a man strikes thee on thy right cheek,
turn the other cheek toward him;
if he is ready to go to law with thee
over thy coat,
let him have it and thy cloak with it;
if he compels thee to attend him
on a mile's journey,
go two miles with him
of thy own accord.

Matthew 5:38-42 Knox

His

It doesn't take too much planning or energy to return equal for equal—a bad deed for a bad deed or a good deed for a good deed. Quite often homelife seems to be based upon this simplistic equation: an equal for an equal. Unfortunately, some men even slight the equality of good deeds in the home. They seem to think they can get away with doing little or nothing since their continual good deed is bringing home a healthy paycheck. "I've done my duty. Why should I do any more for my wife than she does for me?"

It's a human tendency to measure the deeds one does in accordance to what others have done toward him. If a wife does something especially good for her husband, he doesn't find it difficult to make a response. On other occasions, the husband performs a good deed mainly to keep peace between himself and his wife.

But the idea of turning the other cheek, giving a cloak, walking a second mile—these are strange propositions for the Lord to make—even in the husband/wife setting. Isn't He really talking about one's relationship to persons outside of the family?

Does a situation ever arise in which a wife strikes one cheek? is ready to go to law for a man's coat? or compels him to take a one-mile hike? Not if the man and wife are on good terms. Not if their motivation in their homelife is genuine Christian love. Not if each does good deeds without an "equal-for-equal" motive.

But no situation meets the perfect ideal, so a man ought to know how (and be willing!) to turn his head, take off his cloak, and even put on his hiking shoes!

Hers

Let's look at this two-mile hike in the literal sense. Couple it with the knowledge that differences do arise in every home. Occasionally a husband gets angry with his wife. Occasionally a wife becomes quite frustrated with her husband. The Lord suggested an extremely practical method for repairing broken or aggravated relationships—put on your shoes, get out of the house, take a long walk!

Getting off the premises for a short period of time isn't a bad idea. Taking a leisurely walk together in which each partner deliberately "cools off" sounds like an excellent piece of advice. The Lord, who did a lot of walking, knew the therapeutic values of a good hike.

Maybe a husband will suggest that he and his wife take a "cooling off" walk. A wife can further cool him off by doubling the hike, possibly not in distance, but in purpose. She can set the tone by forgiveness and cooperation. She can mend the broken relationship. She can draw her husband into a sweeter relationship.

A two-mile hike also has refreshing values as husband and wife expand their interest in the world around them. Often we don't see how others live unless we get down to street level. We become so involved in our world that we fail to observe the larger society in which we move—often even less than two miles from our doorsteps.

Two miles really isn't too far to walk if it eliminates frictions between a wife and husband. You really can't be angry with a person with whom you walk hand in hand. It sure was great for Jesus to come up with the two-mile hike idea. Let's go take a hike!

Prayers

HIS

Lord, I realize how much of my life is based upon an "even Stephen" approach—equal for equal. This is true in regard to most of my good deeds. Give me the grace to go out of my way to right wrongs, to do good—particularly to my wife. In the name of the One who was known for doing good. Amen.

HERS

I need to learn the values of a leisurely approach to problem solving and to meeting the demands of my husband. May my attitude coincide with Yours when it comes to dealing with the demands of others. In the name of Him who willingly journeyed the rough road to Calvary. Amen.

LET'S TALK MORE

In what aspects of our lives do we tend to exchange equal-for-equal good deeds? How should this change so we won't put a limit on our doing good? (Possibly this could be discussed on an outdoor hike!)

Having Good Ears

Understand [this], my beloved brethren.
Let every man be quick to hear,
(a ready listener,)
slow to speak,
slow to take offense and to get angry.

James 1:19 Amplified

A wise man
will hear
and increase his learning.

Proverbs 1:5 Berkeley

His

Extrovertish men usually seem ready to comment about life. No matter what the subject, if they have but a little knowledge about it, they offer an opinion. It seems that the average fellow thinks, "Of what value is an opinion locked up in a man's brain?" Opinions need expression, otherwise a choice bit of wisdom might be lost!

We live in an era when it seems more acceptable to express opinions than to keep one's mouth shut. Talking seems to have greater significance than listening. In most organizations a man who only listens is relegated to a back seat. "Speak up, man!" he is urged. So in order to maintain an acceptable position among his peers, a man is often forced to talk, even when he has little to contribute.

In contrast to this is James's exhortation, "Let every man be quick to hear, (a ready listener)." This puts a premium upon listening to an opinion rather than expressing one. This makes the reception of words more important than the speaking of them. Of course, it openly acknowledges that one shall allow others the privilege of doing the speaking. In listening, a man learns how to sift out the important from the frivolous. He learns how to evaluate the words that come to his ears.

In marriage, where a man can readily dominate the situation, listening becomes a prized virtue. "A wise man will hear (even his wife's opinions!) and increase his learning." Listen to her express her desires; listen to her express her faith in Christ; listen to her express the longings of her personality—all these help a man to show love to his mate and to increase his learning.

Hers

Confession No. 1—that tale about gossipy women is too often true. Telephone wires "burn" and time slips by when the housewife holds the mouthpiece. Words come without effort—often unnecessary words about other people. People are the most interesting topics of conversation. So what's the harm of a little talk about them?

When talking about others, it's difficult not to slip from the passing on of legitimate information over to the evil practice of gossiping. Some women have acquired reputations for just that. They spill forth character-damaging words whenever they talk, which is frequently. They know "the latest" about most of their acquaintances, and if they don't, they make it their business to find out.

Yet, even to be able to gossip, a person has to listen in order to receive the information to pass on. It's unfortunate that we have such good ears when evil news is in the air! But thank God that the same ears that listen to the evil news can also receive the news that can compel us to action. Those ears, under the control of the compassionate Christ, can be tuned to hearing the heart cries of the needy, usually expressed in plaintive language. God saw fit to give women sensitive ears when others cry in agony, hunger, or loneliness.

How good to have such ears in the home. To hear the meaning of a husband's words of disappointment, pain, sorrow, disquiet—to hear a call for help when the words and tone may convey anger. To be a ready listener makes a wife so much more compassionate, so much more the helpmeet God intended.

In being a ready listener, a woman has to put into practice the following instruction of James: "Slow to speak, slow to take offense and to get angry." Good ears are an excellent asset, and are even more valuable when coupled with a controlled tongue.

Prayers

HIS

Lord, in this era of almost instant communications, the tensions of life seem to force people into expressing opinions. Give me the wisdom to know when to express thoughts and when to be quiet. You gave me good ears as well as an articulate tongue. Help me to use both at the proper time—and for Your glory. Amen.

HERS

I'm often tempted to put my ears into the affairs of others. Then after my head is full, it seems I need an oral outlet. May I learn to guard that to which I give attention with my ears, and sift carefully that which I should forget from that which I choose to store in my mind, and that which I should speak. Allow me the privilege of being a confidant to those who need the therapy supplied through a good listener. Amen.

LET'S TALK MORE

Do either of us feel the other talks too much? What steps will we take to correct this? How can each of us learn to be better listeners?

Honestly Now

Let your Yes
be simply Yes,
and your No be simply No;
anything more than that
comes from the evil one.

Matthew 5:37 Amplified

His

Indecision and noncommitment seem to be a common, acceptable practice in almost every man's work world. If you don't commit yourself to a position, you can't be blamed if it doesn't work out—"It wasn't *my* idea!"

Even those who are assigned to committees often resort to "Maybe" answers. They avoid a Yes or No answer—then it's easy to pass the buck and they never have to take the blame for anything—although they usually seem to be at the head of the line when praise is given!

But how contrary to the principle presented by Jesus Christ. He said our *Yes* should be a simple, definite Yes; our *No* a simple, definite, meaningful No.

To make such answers we need to know what we are talking about. We need to take into consideration the full consequences of a resounding Yes or an absolute No. And then we need the courage to accept the consequences of each of our decisions. Happy is the man who can say Yes and mean it and say No and stick to it.

What's true in business is also true in the business of marriage. It's often more convenient to be noncommittal, but it's more spiritually and mentally healthy to say Yes or No. A wife will enjoy hearing clearcut replies because such answers are sure to help solve marital problems. It takes a *man* to be so sure!

Hers

Sometimes a wife will complicate her Yes or No answers to tease her husband; sometimes to force him into submission to her desires; sometimes to gain advantage over him. Wives can be clever with the Maybe answers. The Maybe answer often has some pointed values. Often it isn't so much an escape hatch to buck-passing as it is a clever psychological device.

There are times when the ambiguous answer is the only legitimate one. A person might not *know* whether Yes or whether No is the correct response. Then an indefinite answer isn't necessarily wrong and doesn't contradict the principle presented by Christ. Wisdom then dictates the use of this technique until a more firm decision based on better knowledge can be made.

But a wife often uses the indefinite approach when she could easily have given a definite Yes or No. She tests her husband's response. Sometimes his response will be more favorable if she isn't dogmatic in answering. Then she'll gain her desires, which she might not have been able to do if she had given a clear Yes or No to his question.

This, of course, takes a rather short-term view of the values of the indefinite answer. Saying Yes or No without qualifications is geared to the long-term good. Thus a Yes that might produce a present setback might advance future causes. A No today might turn into the best Yes tomorrow shall ever know.

And in the love relationship between husband and wife, a relationship dominated by the love of Christ and based upon mutual trust, simple positive or negative answers build the marriage. Anything beyond this makes for suspicion and eventually tears the relationship apart. How wonderful to be fully honest with one's mate!

Prayers

HIS

I see so much dishonesty around me, so much buck-passing, Lord, that I need inner courage and simplicity to always make clear positive and negative replies. Help me to always say a loud Yes to those positive values in life and an eternally clear No to anything evil. Amen.

HERS

Give me the uncomplicated spirit that says Yes and No rather than the answer-avoiding Maybe. Teach me how to be strictly honest while maintaining an attitude of love. May we grow together in personal and neighborly honesty. Amen.

LET'S TALK MORE

In what areas of life do we usually hedge concerning positive or negative answers? Why? How can we develop the attitude and atmosphere for being totally honest with each other, yet loving toward each other?

Till Death Do Us Part

. . . some Pharisees came up,
and in order to test Him
and try to find a weakness in Him asked,
Is it lawful for a man to dismiss
and repudiate
and divorce his wife?
He answered them,
What did Moses command you?
They replied,
Moses allowed a man to write a bill of divorce,
and to put her away.
But Jesus said to them,
Because of your hardness of heart
[that is, of your condition of
insensibility to the call of God]
he wrote you this precept in your Law.
But from the beginning of creation
God made them male and female.
For this reason
a man shall leave (behind)
his father and his mother
and be joined to his wife,
and cleave closely to her (permanently).

Mark 10:2-7 Amplified

His

No honest Christian man can conclude that present-day divorce practices are a norm by which one has a right to live. Rather, the divine mandate talks about the permanency of marriage. Of course, there's the exception clause allowed by the Lord (see Matthew 19:9). Notice, though, that Jesus said that Moses wrote a divorce law because of the hardness of their hearts, not as an acceptable Christian practice.

But to simply state that permanence in marriage is a Christian doctrine doesn't automatically guarantee an until-death-do-us-part situation for Christian husband/wife partnerships. It takes considerably more than this. We can point to Christian couples we have known who have reluctantly resorted to a divorce court. For some time they possibly had agreed that the Biblical position on divorce was a reason for their not getting a divorce. Yet finally they concluded that divorce was the only escape. The *statement* of the doctrine wasn't sufficient. It always has to be supported by actual *living.*

Jesus pointed out that Moses allowed for divorce because of "your condition of insensibility to the call of God." To the person who becomes insensible (or insensitive) to the call of God—to the call to Christ-controlled living—becoming insensitive to his marriage partner isn't a major step. Stating a doctrine will not keep him from threatening divorce or getting a divorce.

The sanction God put upon the permanent husband/wife situation should be a motivation to what Jesus suggested: "a man shall leave behind his father and his mother and be joined to his wife, and cleave closely to her." If he practices cleaving closely, permanence in marriage will be achieved. How good is God to supply the means for this closeness.

Hers

Divorce is an easy way out! Most people who hire divorce lawyers don't really want to solve marriage problems. They've lived rather selfishly and find divorce a quick escape. It's true, sometimes a person has teamed up with a wandering boy or a man who has chosen to be totally incompatible. But an honest evaluation will usually show that the woman is partly at fault. She possibly neglected to show that love and devotion which would have drawn her husband to herself.

The Christian woman can thank God that there's a better way to solve husband/wife conflicts. Divorce isn't the answer. Rather, God has provided the inner characteristics that help a woman face her marriage problems in the spirit of love.

The grace of God helps a woman cleave closely to a husband in the same manner it helps a husband cleave closely to her. In such a true-love relationship—true love for God and for her husband—a wife never thinks of terminating her marriage. Instead there's a great desire to continue showing love to the husband God has permitted her to have. Only in a lifelong relationship will she be able to show her mate all that God has put into her heart.

Maturing together can be a most satisfying part of life. It takes patience. It takes the sharing of difficulties. It takes the working out of contrary views. To adhere to the Christ-proposed view of marriage makes sense if a woman wants to develop into a complete person.

There's *so* much to a permanent marriage relationship—a truly fulfilling experience for the individuals involved and an example to others of what God intends marriage to be. It's up to each partner to take the responsibility of making permanence an exciting part of their life's journey.

Prayers

HIS

In accepting the marriage plan You advocate, keep me sensitive to the personality of my marriage partner. May the permanence of my vows be a basis for bettering our relationship. May we together show the world that a couple can happily follow Your Law. Amen.

HERS

Thank You for making marriage a permanent relationship, thus adding stability to my life. Keep me sensitive to those aspects of marriage that can make our relationship a highly enjoyable partnership and an example to those around us. May we experience the physical, mental and spiritual richness that comes by cleaving closely to each other. Amen.

LET'S TALK MORE

What are some of the elements of life that force couples apart? How can we keep these elements out of our marriage? How can we help others in whose marriage such elements are present?

Children:
Legacy from the Lord

Behold,
children are a legacy from the Lord;
the fruit of the womb
is His reward.
As arrows in the hand of a mighty man,
so are the children of one's youth.
Blessed is the man
who has his quiver full of them.

Psalm 127:3-5 Berkeley

His

Being a father is a serious matter. Accepting the responsibilities not only for starting a life but for nurturing a child can be frightening in our day. A father often wonders, What will my child become? Will he enjoy the freedoms I now enjoy? Will he be healthy and happy? Will he contribute something worthwhile to society? What if he is a she? How will this affect the way I look upon my offspring? Did I want a boy more than a girl? Will she grow to be like her mother? Would I want her elsewise?

In an era of overpopulation, how seriously should a man take the psalmist's words, "Blessed is the man who has his quiver full of them"? Should a man limit the number of children he brings into the world? Is it a sin to add to the overpopulation of our planet? Should the Christian family be limited to two offspring?

In spite of all the questions we can propose about bringing children into the world, one quickly recognizes that children add depth to married life. Since God put the procreative power within man and that procreative power is released during the highest ecstatic experience of life, surely God meant for marriage partners to become parents. The fulfillment of the God-ordained result of the marriage relationship brings great satisfaction.

Children add much to the home. They challenge a father intellectually and emotionally. He becomes teacher and counselor. He becomes everything the designation "Daddy" calls forth. That is, he does if he wants to do what God intended fathers to do.

Hers

Before marriage a young woman often thinks of having children. She discusses the idea with friends. She considers how many offspring she'd like to bring into the world. She is eager to hear about various types of childbirth. She might even dream about pregnancy's joys and feelings.

When children arrive in the home there's an inner glow no one can explain, not even the new mother herself. It's more than pride. It's a satisfaction that she has produced a new life. She has mothered a child. It's an awesome experience—but one of exciting joy. Truly, as the Psalmist proclaimed, "The fruit of the womb is His reward." She feels rewarded!

As she watches the children grow, she faces new challenges. She faces heartaches as well as joys. Children disobey as well as heed her commands. They squabble as well as play. They argue as well as discuss. Opposite characteristics display themselves—even in one child! So a mother raises children with mixed periods of grief and joy, of disappointment and pride. But that's motherhood—and most mothers wouldn't desire that life be any different.

No matter what attitudes children display, the devoted Christian mother will always look upon her children as a legacy from the Lord. They enrich life. They make a mother's life complete. They provide a means of emotional and spiritual maturity not given to the childless. And as each new child is welcomed into the home, the mother's life takes on a new and thrilling dimension.

How good to have a husband who shares the enrichment children afford to married life. How good to bring children into the world!

Prayers

HIS

Thank You, God, for our children. May I be a most helpful father. May I ever be open to their emotional, intellectual and spiritual needs. May I deserve the name we so reverently apply to You— Father! Amen.

HERS

Forgive me for failing often to see and appreciate the legacy my children have brought to our home. Many times I've been so nearsighted I don't see what good and glory they provide in my life. Thank You, Lord, for the glorious position You have given to me as a mother. In the name of Him who calls us His children. Amen.

LET'S TALK MORE

In what specific ways have our children enriched our lives? How can we more adequately express appreciation for and to them?

Train Up a Child

Educate a child
according to his life requirements;
even when he is old
he will not veer from it.

Proverbs 22:6 Berkeley

These words
with which I am now charging you
shall be written
on your heart;
and you shall impress them deeply
upon your children.

Deuteronomy 6:6, 7 Berkeley

His

Most of us were raised under the concept that parents had the responsibility for clearly hewing out the religious path a child should travel. Thus our parents usually spelled out our beliefs and expected us to adhere to them without questioning. While one can't present too much argument against the content of their beliefs, the method of propagating them can definitely be questioned. Religious experience is far more than the acquisition of religious knowledge.

The pro and con arguments about types of education abound. Traditionalists adhere to content-centered indoctrination. And the King James Version of Proverbs 22:6, "Train up a child in the way he should go" might support this view. But most of today's education, even in the church, is pupil-centered. The Berkeley Version seems to endorse this: "Educate a child *according to his life requirements.*" Look at life and then find the Bibilical principles that apply. Teach what is applicable to life situations.

Fathers have considerable difficulty knowing what are the life requirements of a child. Surely the child should clearly understand how to trust Jesus Christ. He should be led into a strong belief concerning the values of life—that of both others and of himself. He should learn early the dynamic of the Bible as the Word of God. Life should have eternal dimensions. Service should outshine self-interests.

Rather than training a child for a specific occupation, be it religious or secular, parents need to concentrate on character building. If children have adequate inner resources, they will be able to face life's difficult situations and today's moral laxity. Surely such preparation on the part of parents will stabilize the child throughout life.

Hers

Educating a child is a long-term process—a mother knows! How quickly a child seems to forget the lessons of yesterday. It can be so discouraging.

We have a big order from the Lord. Most of us don't really know how to react to all that life seems to require of us, much less how to teach the coming generation how they should react. And since this is a Biblical injunction, we also often limit its application to religious training. The Deuteronomy verses would fortify this considerably—so maybe we ought to give greater attention to the religious knowledge we seek to pack into our children's minds. Is it adequate? Does it lead them to make moral decisions? Has it affected their lives? Are we systematic in the religious training of our children?

A mother often takes the greatest responsibility for the religious education of the children. Why? Mainly because the husband/father excuses himself at this point. He bypasses his duty muttering about his "busyness" as an excuse. He assures himself that his wife is better qualified.

What an awesome task—to educate a child; to lead him or her to study those subjects that will best prepare him for future living; to give the child an adequate Biblical base upon which to build a saving relationship to Jesus Christ that will stand the attacks of secular philosophy; to develop a child's mind in such a way that he'll follow your educational coaching.

What a challenge—to be a part of the process that makes a man out of a boy and a woman out of a girl. To this task a mother gladly dedicates herself.

Prayers

HIS

All-knowing God, give me adequate wisdom to impart both knowledge and eternal principles to my children. Help me to inspire them through my good example. Let them see Christ through my manner of living. Amen.

HERS

Inspire my children to follow You because I follow You, Lord. Keep my goals for them clear in my thinking so I'll be able to direct them in life's important requirements. Thank You for what they've already learned that is preparing them for mature approaches to living. Amen.

LET'S TALK MORE

Name several of the basic requirements a child needs in order to face life victoriously. How are we helping him to develop these?

To Be Continued

I will bless the Lord
at all times;
His praise shall
continually be in my mouth.

Psalm 34:1 Berkeley

Through Jesus, then,
let us continually offer
up to God
the sacrifice of praise,
that is,
the tribute of lips which acknowledge his name,
and never forget
to show kindness
and to share what you have with others;
for such are the sacrifices
which God approves.

Hebrews 13:15, 16 NEB

His

It has been good to review a man's relationship to his wife by seeing some of what the Bible has said about various aspects of the husband/wife situation. The devotional experience is a vital part of that relationship. These devotionals have enriched the marriage relationship. But coming to the end of this book should not limit the number of challenging encounters a man has with his wife. It need not be so. You can continue on your own.

The psalmist said, "I will bless the Lord at all times; His praise shall continually be in my mouth." This can be true for any man today, but it takes effort. God's praise can abound in any home. A husband/wife team can "continually offer up to God the sacrifice of praise, that is, the tribute of lips which acknowledge his name."

If the devotional attitudes developed during the use of these twenty-two devotionals are to be continued, two approaches can be taken. First, reread them. That would be excellent. Surely every possible point has not been covered on the themes discussed. Beyond this, the attitudes developed need reexamination and expansion.

The most valuable approach would be to establish a devotional period based on the pattern developed here. The husband/wife team that continues to take both a male and female look at Biblical texts and says to each other, "Let's talk more," have gained the greatest good from these pages.

How good to manfully proclaim, "I will bless the Lord at all times." How good to do it hand in hand with a wife who discusses with you the Word of God and also applies it to her daily living.

Hers

To close this book and go back to child-oriented devotionals would be a step backwards. Thus we must continue. This is suggested both in the Psalm and in Hebrews. To enhance life by sharing devotional thoughts ought to be one of the primary goals of a Christian couple. How good to discuss the Bible in relationship to married life. How exciting! How challenging! How demanding!

To have praise to God continually in one's thoughts and upon one's lips is a high goal. It's not easily reached. In the husband/wife relationship, a wife finds some good opportunities to praise God. But some encounters do not promote praise; they inspire complaint. Honesty requires that we acknowledge this also.

Both husband and wife have to be honest when applying Biblical truths to marriage. Lacking honesty, the application of these truths can easily disgress into accusation. Discussing the most intimate subjects in relationship to Biblical truths demands an openness of mind and spirit. It challenges both husband and wife to an expansion of personal views.

In these devotionals we have discussed subjects rarely touched upon, especially in relationship to God's Word and will. Understanding where God fits into a marriage enriches the Christian aspect of the marriage union. We can say, "Thank You for joining us together."

To be continued. That's every wife's hope when something exciting and worthwhile has been developed. So here's a pattern. Take new texts, look at them in a similar manner, and then challenge yourselves with soul-searching and honest inquiry. To be continued— so that God can continue the good work He has been performing in these days.